Thasos: ten centuries inscribed in marble

A brief history on the basis of inscriptions

Julien FOURNIER, Patrice HAMON, Natacha TRIPPÉ

ÉCOLE FRANÇAISE D'ATHÈNES
ΓΑΛΛΙΚΗ ΣΧΟΛΗ ΑΘΗΝΩΝ

A Foreword by the Authors

The inscriptions below are presented only in translation. Those who wish to read the original Greek text should refer to the bibliographic reference cited for each document. Following the standard conventions for the publication of epigraphic documents, we use square brackets in the translation to indicate that the inscribed text contains a more or less extensive lacuna, restored or not (eg. **17** : '*Of King Phili[p] Saviour*'); parentheses are used to explain a word implied or to provide precision (eg **23**: '*The People (honoured) Sextus Pompeius*').

The sign ★ refers to the plans of the territory, the ancient city and the agora on which the location of each monument is indicated. Each inscription is also indicated by its number, at least when its original location is precisely known. The sign ☞ indicates that the inscription is exhibited in one of the rooms of the museum or is still visible on the site. Asterisks (*) refer to the lexicon (p. 59).

Bibliographic Abbreviations

BCH = Bulletin de correspondance hellénique.

CITh III = P. HAMON, *Corpus des inscriptions de Thasos, III. Documents publics du IVᵉ siècle et de l'époque hellénistique, ÉtThas* XXVI (2019).

IG XII 8 = C. FREDRICH, *Inscriptiones Insularum Maris Aegaei praeter Delum VIII : Inscriptiones Insularum Maris Thracici* (1909).

IG XII *Suppl.* = Fr. HILLER VON GAERTRINGEN, *Inscriptiones Insularum Maris Aegaei praeter Delum, Supplementum* (1939).

Recherches I = J. POUILLOUX, *Recherches sur l'histoire et les cultes de Thasos*, I, *ÉtThas* III (1954).

Recherches II = Chr. DUNANT, J. POUILLOUX, *Recherches sur l'histoire et les cultes de Thasos*, II, *ÉtThas* V (1958).

SEG = Supplementum Epigraphicum Graecum.

Chronology

Archaic period

***c.*670 BC**: foundation of the city of Thasos by Parian settlers.

7th–6th c.: gradual takeover of the mainland coast (the 'peraia*').

Classical period

494–491 BC: construction of the city-walls; in **492**, Thasos pledges allegiance to the Persian King Darius.

480–479: Second Persian War; freed from the Persians, Thasos becomes in 477 a member of the Athenian Alliance ('Delian League').

465–463: Thasos leaves the Athenian Alliance; the city is besieged by Cimon; the Thasians capitulate and submit to the Athenians.

431–404: Peloponnesian War between Athens and Sparta; Thasos serves as a naval base for the Athenians.

411–407: establishment of an oligarchy; revolt against Athens; Hippocrates stays in Thasos.

407–405: brief restoration of Athenian hegemony; in **405**, the Spartan Lysander wins an ultimate victory over Athens and establishes the hegemony of Sparta at Thasos.

390: expulsion of the Lacedaemonian garrison; restoration of democracy.

*c.***375**: Thasos becomes a member of the Second Athenian League, a maritime confederation of Aegean city-states.

360–356: secession of the 'Thasians of the mainland' established at Krenides/Datos; loss of the peraia* to Philip II, king of Macedonia.

338: Battle of Chaeronea; Thasos rallies to Philip II in **337**.

Hellenistic period

334–325 BC: Alexander the Great conquers the Persian empire.

323–*c.***280**: emergence of the major Graeco-Macedonian kingdoms in the East; in the 3rd c., Thasos is allied to the Antigonid kingdom; trade of Thasian wine to the Black Sea flourishes.

202–197: Thasos is defeated and occupied by Philip V of Macedonia.

196: the Romans free Thasos from Macedonian hegemony.

89–86: Mithridates, king of Pontus, invades Asia Minor, then Greece; Thasos is besieged, but withstands him.

42: Battle of Philippi; Thasos sides with the assassins of Caesar, Brutus and Cassius.

Imperial period

27 BC: foundation of the Principate*; beginning of a long period of peace in Thasos.

AD 46: creation of the Roman province of Thrace.

96–192: dynasty of the Antonines; urban development on a large scale in Thasos.

293: foundation of the Tetrarchy by Diocletian; Thasos is again attached to the Roman province of Macedonia.

306–363: Constantinian dynasty; last public inscriptions of the city of Thasos.

380: Edict of the Emperor Theodosius banning pagan cults; first Christian monuments in Thasos.

Introduction

Ancient Greek cities were small communities, attached to their identity and their history. Each had its own laws (oligarchic or democratic), managed its own affairs and its own cults, defended its own territory and was in charge of its own finances. Its citizens met in assembly to make decisions; the magistrates, elected or chosen by lot, were in charge of the day-to-day running of government. The institutional machinery produced a large number of decrees, accounts and diplomatic acts, which were preserved on papyrus in the public archives. Moreover, from the Classical period (5th to 4th centuries BC) onwards, it became common practice to inscribe certain texts on marble or bronze and to display them in public. This practice, described as 'epigraphic' – from the Greek word *epigraphein*, 'to write upon' – is known from elsewhere in the Mediterranean, but is particularly developed in Greece. The work of engraving was entrusted to a specialized craftsman, the letter cutter, and was expensive. It was therefore reserved for a small proportion of all documents, those considered to be important. The aim was to bring these documents to everyone's attention, to glorify common values, important events, or remarkable individuals, to show the allegiance of the city to a higher power, to counter indifference or oblivion. On an individual level, too, inscriptions were commissioned to preserve for posterity a pious gesture or the name of a deceased person, or to advertise wealth and family pride.

Located on an island in the Aegean Sea, a stone's throw from the Thracian mainland, Thasos is a perfect example of a Greek city. Founded in the 7th century BC by settlers from Paros (an island in the Cyclades), it has a long and distinguished history. Controlling the island and, intermittently, a part of the coastline facing it (the peraia*), with an excellent port and multiple resources, the city was rich and powerful in the Archaic period (7th–6th centuries BC). In the Classical period, Thasos had to submit to the authority of two Aegean powers, Athens and then the kingdom of Macedonia, before entering, in the 2nd century BC, into an alliance with Rome. Among the riches that made its fortune, Thasos possessed marble quarries and the Thasians were masters in the art of quarrying, cutting and sculpting stone. It is no surprise then that they also engraved many inscriptions. The excavations conducted from 1911 by the French Archaeological School, and nowadays in close collaboration with the Greek Ephorate of Antiquities, have uncovered nearly 2,000 inscriptions, complete or fragmentary. Most come from the agora, the beating heart of the city. Regulations, honorific decrees, dedications of statues, etc. were inscribed and set up there. In other parts of the city there were sanctuaries devoted to the deities of the local pantheon: the Herakleion, which was the hub of Thasian life, the Pythion, the Dionysion or the Artemision, where sacrificial regulations and ex-votos were inscribed and set up. Several further areas have produced inscriptions, public or private: the city-walls, the port, the theatre and lastly the necropoleis outside the walls. Beyond the city, the island territory was dotted with villages and sanctuaries, but these have yielded few inscriptions.

The ancient monuments of Thasos were destroyed in the Protobyzantine period (5th–7th centuries AD) to serve as building material, with as a result that many inscriptions have come to us as fragments. In order to edit them, it is first necessary to decipher the text and, if it is damaged, to reconstitute it as closely as possible to its original state by putting together the fragments, determining the extent of any gaps and proposing plausible restorations. To establish a chronology, we rely on externally dateable facts or individuals, and on the analysis of the language and alphabet used by the author, as well as on the 'paleography', that is the way in which the stonemason drew the letters. Since excavations began, several generations of epigraphists have published or republished the inscriptions of Thasos and have thus progressively enriched our knowledge. Combined with literary, archaeological and numismatic sources, epigraphy provides a great deal of information about the city: not only about political, diplomatic and military events, but also law, production and trade, society, relations between men and women and between free men and slaves, as well as about culture, the gods and Thasian identity.

The aim of this small book is not to be a complete historical narrative, nor a visitor's guide, but to offer a chronological overview of Thasian epigraphy, mixing the various categories of documents and explaining in passing a number of features of this type of source material. The reader is invited to venture, from inscription to the next, into some ten centuries of Thasian history.

Thasos: ten centuries inscribed in marble.

The Thasian construction of Time: monumental lists from the agora

The Thasians cared about the preservation of their past. In the works of the Parian poet Archilochus (*c.*680–640 BC) they could read about the colonial adventure that gave birth to their city. But it is probable that they themselves too wrote their own history, though the shape they gave it and the methods they used are not those that we use today. This local historiography, made up of stories in prose and verse, is now entirely lost. Even so, a remarkable documentary source that has no real equivalent elsewhere in the Greek world survives in the form of two large chronological lists, inscribed, from the fourth century BC onwards, on buildings in the agora. These lists record the incumbents of the two main annual magistracies of Thasos: the three archons*, who constituted the senior executive, and the three *theoroi**, who supervised the cults. The lists begin in the Archaic period, shortly after the founding of Thasos by the Parians (*c.*670 BC), and then continue, column after column, until the Severan period (AD *c.*230). From generation to generation the same names recur, which shows that these prestigious positions were held by a small number of families. We can estimate that, in their final state, the two catalogues totalled respectively about 2,500, and 2,000 individual names, offering an impressive visual record. We have here a perfect example of the social construction of memory: in order to consolidate and glorify its identity, a community – the city of Thasos – creates an image of its past. Standing before these monumental marble annals each citizen could locate himself in time, assess at a glance the number of years he had lived, and even perhaps identify his ancestors' place in the columns that preceded him. Taken as a whole, these inscribed lists constituted both an eloquent and a living – because continuously evolving – picture of the long history of the Thasians.

The lists were uncovered in the excavations of the agora, in varying degrees of fragmentation. They form a gigantic puzzle, full of gaps, and therefore uncertainties continue. Incomplete though it is, this assemblage is of paramount importance, for it provides the backbone of Thasian history over a period of almost nine centuries.

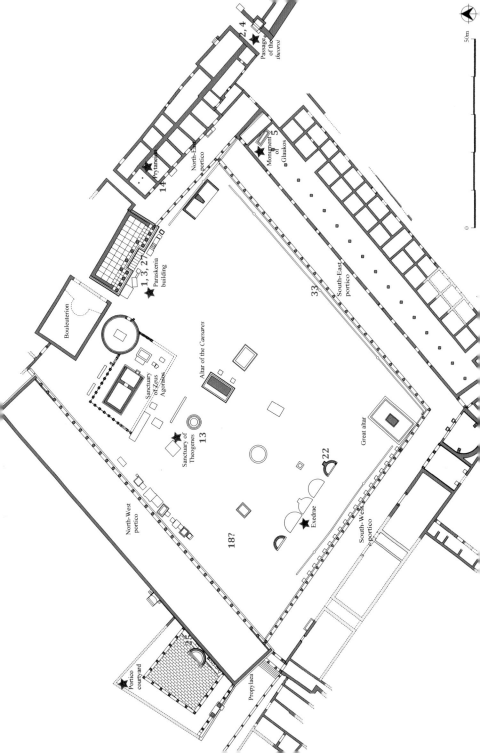

Passage of the *theoroi*

2, 4

Monument of Glaukos

5

North-East portico

Prytaneion

14

Paraskenia building

1, 3, 21

South-East portico

33

Boulenterion

Sanctuary of Zeus Agoraios

Altar of the *Caesares*

Sanctuary of Theogenes

13

Great altar

22

North-West portico

Exedrae

18?

South-West portico

Portico courtyard

Propylaea

N

0   50m

Pythiphon son of Amphikrates.
Aristophanes son of Andron
Lykos son of Archon
Brithon son of Nymphis.
Tellis son of Times
Pankratides son of Erasis
Hegesiboulos son of Lydos.
Brattides son of Deillos
Ideratos son of Nikon
Philanthos son of Andramides.
Leokrates son of Athenades
Leomedon son of Konon
Semonides son of Megylles.
Akeratos son of Phrasierides
Thrason son of Polyon
Simias son of Times.

[.]the[. .]mi[- - - - - - -].
Hegesarchos son of Megon
Kallimedes son of Thrasys
Thersenor son of Nauson.
Lykophron son of Kleokritos
Habronax son of Pankratides
Anaxis son of Orthagores.
Demokrates son of Kydenor
Timesidikos son of Arimnestos
Damnis son of Aristonymos.
Hippokrates son of Eperatos
Aristopolis son of Demosthenes
Leophanes son of Timokrates.
Aristopolis son of Kratis
Deinokles son of Pankratides
Pankratides son of Chrysoros

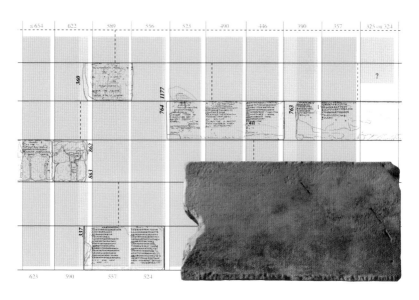

This block belongs to the List of archons*, which was inscribed *c*.360 BC on a white marble wall whose original location is not known. Groups of three names are separated from each other by a dash on the left. The block is located at the bottom of columns 3 and 4, in theory covering the dates ± 562–557 and ± 529–524 BC. The names, which show great variation, are formed from Greek words indicating excellence, power, leadership, fame, horse, etc. They reflect the thought-world of the Archaic Thasian elite, its Parian cultural heritage, its tastes and aristocratic values. Among them we find that of Akeratos son of Phrasierides, an important person from the mid-6th century. He is known through a dedication from the Herakleion (**6**) as well as from his funerary monument. For some reason, this List of archons* was discontinued after about forty years, *c*.320 BC. The Thasians decided to reinscribe it in its entirety on another building, of grey marble, in larger and more visible letters. There are thus two copies of the same list.

2 Hellenistic and Imperial additions (excerpt)
Recherches II, 204

(**B**) *Philippos son of Herodes*
Persaios son of Apollonios
Philippos son of Neikanor.

(**A**) *Corn(elius) Stratokles*
Titus Aur(elius) Leonas
priest of Dionysos

(**C**) *Parthenios son of Parthenios*
Archeleos son of Heragoras
Paramonos son of Paramonos

Flavius Vale-
rius Paramonos
High-[priest ?].

(**D**) *P[- -]*

Thasos: ten centuries inscribed in marble.

The second version of the List of archons*, inscribed on grey marble, contains, first, a recapitulative section (up to *c.*320 BC), then an additional part, which was completed over the years, during the Hellenistic period and the beginning of the imperial period. By the middle of the first century AD, the Thasians abandoned the principle of inscribing in regular columns, but continued to inscribe the names of the archons* in the remaining empty spaces. This irregular habit, combined with the small number of blocks that survive, further complicates the reconstruction of the chronology for this period. However, we owe it some beautiful examples of the juxtaposition of very different hands, sometimes as far apart as a century or more. The triads **B** and **C**, which are contemporary, date from the second half of the first century AD. They contain ancient names, that go back generations. The archons* of the left triad (**A**), inscribed in a decorative frame of Roman origin (*tabula ansata*), belong to the third century AD, a time when it was not uncommon for additional titles such as priesthoods to be mentioned. Their names reveal that they all possessed Roman citizenship. At the bottom right of the block is the first letter of another name, belonging to a triad that continued on adjacent blocks.

3 Recapitulative List of *theoroi** (excerpt)
IG XII 8, 276, ll. 4-12

At the time
when the Three Hundred and Sixty
were in power,
these were theoroi:

> *Pamphilos son of Ithypolis*
> *Ilis son of Deialkos*
> *Andron son of Choiron.*
> *Harpakos son of Tynnos*
> *Spithamaios son of Alexides*
> *Hippon son of Choiron.*
> *Krinis son of Hegillos*
> *[- - - - - - - - - - - - -]*

Parallel to the List of archons*, a List of *theoroi** was inscribed and set up in the agora, *c.*360 BC: one of its blocks is displayed in the museum (☞ Room 6).

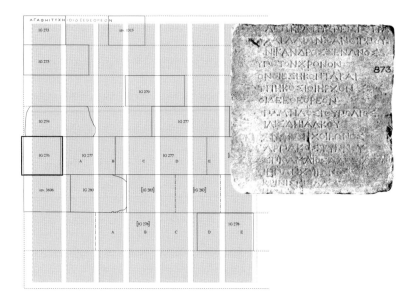

Like that of the archons*, it was discontinued *c*.320 and a second copy was set up in a very busy location: the 'Passage of the *theoroi*'(★), which connects the agora to the Artemision and the Dionysion. This is the best preserved of the large Thasian lists. The extract presented here comes from column 1, towards the middle of the sixth century BC (tentatively ± 544–542). Exceptionally, a subtitle informs us about the city's internal political history: a new regime, known as the 'Three Hundred and Sixty,' had just come into being, perhaps after the fall of a tyrant*. No other source enlightens us about this episode, but the list shows that on this occasion the college of *theoroi** changed to three annual members, conforming to the model of the archons*.

4 Hellenistic and Imperial additions (excerpt)
IG XII 8, 326

Aulus Seius Antigonos,
also called Perigenes.

> *Ktesiphon son of Aristokrates*
> *Posidonios son of Aristokrates*

Nemonios son of Ktesiphon.

Seuthes son of Theogenes

Dionysios
son of Amyntas.

The new List of *theoroi** continued after 320 BC for several centuries. As for the List of archons*, additional columns were added first, then, in the imperial period, the list lost its original order: the names were no longer inscribed in regular columns, nor even in triads. In this fragment of the list, dated towards the beginning of the second century AD, we observe the same decorative motifs as on the late additions to the List of archons*. Traditional names remain numerous, reflecting the ancestral values of the Thasian aristocracy. These traditions, however, had to be relaxed and were reluctantly opened up to newcomers, especially rich freedmen of Roman families. Such was probably the social status of Aulus Seius Antigonos, who, with Seuthes son of Theogenes, also appears in the List of archons*, which indicates that the same men often went on to assume both positions. Nemonios son of Ktesiphon is the father of a philosopher who was honoured by the city (**30**).

The early days of the city (7th–5th centuries BC)

The city of Thasos was founded *c.*670 BC by settlers from the island of Paros, attracted to the region by its mineral wealth. The island was at that time probably occupied by Thracians and bore the name *Odonis* – perhaps related to the tribe of the *Edones*. As in any Archaic colonial enterprise, the expedition was led by an oikist*, Telesikles, himself guided by a pronunciation of the Delphic oracle to 'found on the misty island a city that can be seen from afar.' Some twenty years later, the Parians sent a second contingent to Thasos, which included the poet Archilochus, son of Telesikles. The Thasians owe many essential elements of their identity to their Parian origins: their main cults, their institutions, their personal names, etc. We know almost nothing of the events of the 7th and 6th centuries (**3**), but we can guess that within a few generations, Thasos became a prosperous city. The Thasians gradually established their hegemony over the coast opposite the island and took control of its gold and silver resources. The city developed its trade with the Thracian interior and with the rest of the Greek world. At the beginning of the 5th century, when Thasos submitted to the authority of the Persian King Darius, the city possessed a fleet, and imposing walls, and struck silver coins. Then begins an eventful period in the city's history. In 480, Thasos welcomed the troops of Xerxes, on their march to conquer Greece. A few months later, the Persians were defeated; in 477, Thasos joined, like most cities in the Aegean, the Delian League, a military alliance led by Athens. But relations between the allied Thasians and Athenians quickly deteriorated. In 465, Thasos attempted to escape the hegemony of Athens by

withdrawing from the League. The city was besieged and capitulated after two years, at the price of heavy reprisals: dismantling of the walls, loss of the fleet and the peraia*, and changes to her institutions. From 431 to 404, Athens fought Sparta in the Peloponnesian War. These were dark days for the Thasians, tossed as they were between two camps: they went over to the Spartan side in 411, then again in 405; conflicts between factions and successive revolutions weakened the city for a long time.

Famous visitors passed through the island between the 7th and the 5th centuries – the poet Archilochus, the historians Herodotus and Thucydides, the physician Hippocrates – and provide us with valuable information on political events, the climate and the city's resources. But it is above all epigraphy which, through its variety and its originality, reveals the initial developments of the city. Thasian inscriptions constitute a collection which is particularly rich for the Archaic period, with laws on trade and public order, religious regulations and epitaphs. Until about 420 BC, these texts were written in the Parian alphabet, inherited from the mother city: similar, apart from a few variants, to that used in the Ionian city of Miletus. At this time there was not yet a common Greek language, but there were different regional dialects. In Thasos, the Paro-Thasian dialect, which belongs to the Ionian group, was used.

5 Glaukos, the beautiful Parian, and the foundation of Thasos (late 7th century?) ☞ Room 6
BCH 79 (1955), pp. 75-86

Of Glaukos son of Leptines I am the monument. The sons of Brentes erected me.

This inscription is the oldest known in Thasos. The block that carries it belongs to a funerary monument which is still visible in the agora, not far from the Passage of the *theoroi* (★). The text, in the Parian alphabet, is inscribed *boustrophedon-*style, which is characteristic of the oldest inscriptions: the writing goes from left to right, then, in the following line, from right to left, 'as the ox turns the plough'. As was the custom in the Archaic period, the monument speaks in the first person. The deceased is an important person in Thasian history: Glaukos belongs to the generation of the founders who were celebrated as heroes. He took part in the second Parian expedition, in the company of his friend Archilochus – who describes him in his poems as a man 'with beautiful curly hair' and valiant

in combat. He fell in battle, perhaps facing the Thracians from the mainland. For this reason, he received, around 600 BC, the honour of a cenotaph in a key location, in front of a gate that possibly separated the lower and the upper town and which, a century later, was included in the enlarged circuit of the city walls. The monument of this proud warrior retained, until a much later date, its role as a place of memory for the Thasian community.

6 Akeratos, a great figure of the 6th century (*c.*550–530)
IG XII *Suppl.* 412

Akeratos consecrated me to Heracles, he who alone was in command over the united Thasians and Parians, and who, in charge of many missions for his city, traversed the nations of men – testimony of his eternal valour.

The author of this dedication, Akeratos, is known from two other inscriptions: the List of archons* (**1**) and an epigram inscribed on his funerary monument, a lighthouse built at the entrance to the bay of Potamia on the east coast of the island (★). The imposing dimensions of this base (1.74 × 1.20 m) suggest that it supported a prestigious offering, probably a statue, dedicated to Heracles. The text is written in verse and borrows formulas from epic poetry to praise the feats of the dedicator. Akeratos carried out diplomatic missions in the name of his city and served, perhaps during an expedition on the mainland, as commander of combined Parian-Thasian troops – a feat whose exceptional character he emphasizes. His dedication is a mark of piety towards the deity, but at the same time an ostentatious gesture. Heracles was indeed the tutelary god of the Thasians (**7** and **11**) and his sanctuary was a privileged place for setting up dedications, intended to be seen and to recall the prestige of the dedicator. The sculptural and architectural fragments found in the Herakleion (★), which can now be admired in the museum (☞ Room 10), are among the most beautiful

The early days of the city (7th–5th centuries BC)

examples of Archaic art on Thasos. They confirm the centrality of this sanctuary in the urban landscape and in the religious life of the city. This dedication is a further example of the sanctuary's importance: the care with which the text is inscribed, the choice of the poetic form, and the monumental character of the base, single out the dedication of Akeratos, an Archaic Thasian notable, as a remarkable work.

7 A vase offered to Heracles (2nd half of the 6th century)
M. LAUNEY, *Le sanctuaire et le culte d'Héraklès à Thasos*, *ÉtThas* I (1944), p. 91, n° 1

The handle of this black glaze table amphora dates from the 6th century. It was discovered in the excavations of the Herakleion (★), inside the oldest building of the sanctuary, which consisted of banqueting halls where meat was consumed after the sacrifice. It bears an inscription whose only legible word,

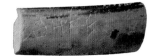

damaged at the beginning, is [AN]EΘHKE (*[an]etheke*), a verb conjugated in the third person singular, which means '[So-and-so] dedicated'. The owner of the vase certainly offered to Heracles the object that he had used at the banquet. In the Archaic period, inscriptions on stone are rare: this is why inscriptions on vases, which we call 'graffiti', are instructive. In these private documents, letters sometimes have shapes that are not used in official inscriptions: here for example, the second letter, *theta* (Θ), does not have a dot in the centre (as in **8** and **9**), but a cross. Since they are so varied (letters, shopping lists, alphabets, dedications, messages of love, etc.), graffiti allow us to enter into the daily life of the ancient Greeks.

8 The sorrow of a mother (*c.*540–510)
IG XII 8, 395

For Thrasykles son
of Pantagathos,
his mother has erected
this tomb.

The Thasian necropoleis lay outside the city, before the gates and along the roads that ran out from them. It is here that was found the funerary stele which marked, at the end of the 6th century, the location of the tomb of Thrasykles, son of Pantagathos. The name of the young man, evoking courage (*thrasos*) and fame (*kleos*), suggests that he belonged to an aristocratic family. Despite the modest dimensions and the oblique script, the stele shows that special care was taken: the text is in verse; the layout of the inscription as well as the smoothing of the surface suggest that

The early days of the city (7th–5th centuries BC)

a decoration was painted on the upper part. To this son, who died prematurely, his mother, whose name remains unknown, wished in this way to offer a last testimony of her love.

9 Order and cleanliness in the streets of Thasos (*c*.480–460) ☞ Room 7
H. DUCHÊNE, *La stèle du port, ÉtThas.* XIV (1992), pp. 19-20, ll. 23-49

(...) From the sanctuary of Heracles to the sea, the epistatai* *are to supervise the cleanliness of the street. What comes out (?) of the houses and what lies on the street is to be removed, whenever the magistrates order it. He who does not act in accordance with the prescriptions shall pay one* hekte* *per day to the city. The* epistatai* *are to exact this and keep half for themselves. On the roofs of the public houses (?) that are located in this street, no one shall go up to look (*or: to be seen*) nor shall any woman look out of (*or: show herself at*) the windows. If he commits any of these offences, the person resident shall pay each time a* stater* *to the city. The* epistatai* *are to exact this and keep half for themselves. From the balcony, no water must be thrown. Whoever does so shall pay a half-*hekte* *per day, half to the city and half to the* epistatai*. *The* epistatai* *are to exact it. – From the sanctuary of the Charites to the buildings housing the exchange office and the banqueting hall, and following the street that runs past the* prytaneion*, *in the middle of this space, garbage must not be thrown and prostitutes must not work the street. Whoever commits one of these offences shall pay each time, as often as the offence is committed, a half-*hekte* *to the city. The* epistatai* *are to exact it and keep half for themselves. Otherwise, they shall pay double to Artemis Hecate.*

Thasos: ten centuries inscribed in marble

This regulation, exceptional both in length and in precision, contains instructions relating to the use of public space. The inscription, very worn from having been submersed in the sea for a considerable time, is written in the Parian alphabet and in the *boustrophedon*-style (**5**). Sometime after it was inscribed, an insensitive passer-by incised a graffito of a helmeted head on the space left free at the bottom of the stele. The passage presented here concerns two sectors of the city. The first is the street that runs from the Herakleion (★) to the sea, probably passing through the Fish Gate (★). The second is a space bordered by the sanctuary of the Charites (or Graces), which was perhaps located in the Passage of the *theoroi* (★), by two civic buildings and by the street along the *prytaneion**: this could well be the agora (★). The regulation aims first at combating poor sanitation by preventing any form of encroachment onto the public domain and by prohibiting the discharge of waste water and the throwing out of garbage onto the streets. It also seeks to maintain public order: it is forbidden to climb onto the roofs and, for women, to 'look' out of the windows; this clause, difficult to interpret, seems to target prostitution and more specifically soliciting. Like any other Greek city, Thasos was anxious to emphasize the difference between courtesans and citizens' wives. A century later, driven by the same concern, the Thasians established *gynaikonomoi**, a board of magistrates responsible for supervising the public conduct of the citizens' wives (**19**). The *epistatai**, who can be compared to a police force with extended responsibilities, are here in charge of enforcing the rules. With its topographical indications, this inscription also allows us to glimpse the broad outlines of the urban landscape of Thasos in the 5th century.

10 Three stops on the road around the island
(*c.*450) ☞ Room 13
BCH 88 (1964), pp. 267-287

> *From the city to here, through Ainyra:*
> *13,660 orgyiai (= c.24.5 km).*
> *From here to the Diasion located in Demetrion:*
> *10,950 orgyiai (= c.20 km).*
> *From the Diasion to the city, along the sea:*
> *19[500?] (Or: 19[050?]) orgyiai (= c.34 km).*

The early days of the city (7th–5th centuries BC)

This marker stone was on display in the sanctuary of Apollo at Aliki (★), on the south-eastern side of the island. It indicates, from the place where it was set up, the distances in *orgyiai* (1 *orgyia* = *c*.1.8 m) separating landmarks in the territory of Thasos. Thus a 78 km-long circuit is outlined: from the ancient city (now Limenas) to Aliki via Ainyra (perhaps located at the exit of Potamia Bay); from Aliki to the Diasion (a sanctuary of Zeus), which was located at a place called Demetrion; and lastly from the Diasion to the city. This is a very remarkable example of a distance marker, one of the oldest known in the Greek world, well before the milestones that later marked the roads of the Roman Empire. The inscription proves that, from the Archaic period onwards, the Thasians travelled all over their island, following a route dotted with villages and shrines, through a rural territory that was closely linked to the urban centre.

11 How to sacrifice to Heracles? (*c.* 440-430)
IG XII *Suppl.* 414

To Thasian Heracles, it is not allowed (to sacrifice) either a goat or a piglet; nor are women allowed (to participate); one does not take the ninth part; one does not cut (priestly) perquisites; no contests are held.

This stele was found re-used near the Passage of the *theoroi* (★). The text uses the Parian alphabet and the inscriber chose the checkerboard layout called *stoichedon*,

which was not uncommon in the 5th century. This regulation belongs to the category of 'sacred laws', which prescribe the details of cultic service rendered to a god. Heracles is one of the oldest and most important deities of the Thasian pantheon. His sanctuary, the Herakleion, benefited, from the 6th century onwards, from exceptional facilities (**6**) and was, together with the Artemision, one of the two centres around which the urban landscape was structured. The fact that this stele was not found in

Thasos: ten centuries inscribed in marble

the Herakleion, but near the agora, might indicate that Heracles had a second place of worship in this area. Using negative clauses, the regulation summarizes the modes of sacrifice to 'Thasian' Heracles, which are different from those practised in the larger sanctuary: in particular, it is here forbidden to burn the ninth part of the victim, which suggests that Heracles was honoured in this place as a god, and not as a hero. If the person sacrificing respected these measures, he would not risk antagonizing the god. Like other texts of the same type, of which there are many in Thasos, the inscription shows that the civic authorities took great care to regulate cult practice.

12 The Thasian families and their gods (c.450–430) ☞ Room 10
BCH 89 (1965), pp. 441-442, n° 1

> *(Boundary marker of the sanctuary) of Zeus* Alastoros Patroios
> *(belonging to the* patre*) of* the Phastadai.

The community of Thasian citizens was subdivided into family groups, called *patrai*, and each *patre* took its name from a heroic ancestor. This stele was found at Evraiokastro (★), at the northern tip of the city – a place identified as the sanctuary of Demeter *Thesmophoros* and today occupied by a charming chapel. Ten other stelae of the same type were discovered there. Each stele marked the site of a sacred enclosure, where the *patre* worshipped its protecting deity. The *Phastadai* placed themselves under the protection of an 'ancestral' (*Patroios*) and 'avenging' (*Alastoros*) Zeus. At l. 2, the name of Zeus is not written ΔΙΟΣ (*Dios*, in the genitive, the possessive case: 'of Zeus'), as it would be in Athens and in most Greek cities, but ΔΙΩΣ (Dios) with a Ω (*omega*), which is one of the characteristic features of the Parian alphabet.

The early days of the city (7th–5th centuries BC)

Between Athens and Macedonia
(4th-2nd centuries BC)

The transition from the 5th to the 4th century BC constitutes a rupture in the history of the city. From 411 onwards, and for more than thirty years subsequently, the Thasians were torn apart, some supporting Athens, others Sparta. Civil war, foreign occupation and repeated coups led to a series of massacres and exiles, followed by returns. Stability was not regained until 375 when, allied once more to Athens, Thasos began to rebuild itself, adopting democratic institutions (probably less radical than those in Athens) and restoring its control over the mainland, the key to flourishing trade with the Thracian world. The new silver coinage with the types of Dionysus and Heracles symbolizes this renewal. The 4th century is also a golden age for Thasian epigraphy. On the agora and in the sanctuaries, numerous regulations, public contracts and dedications were inscribed. This is the time when the Thasians designed their recapitulative lists of magistrates (**1** and **3**), to which they regularly added new entries. The evolution of letter forms, the disappearance of the *stoichedon* style (**11**), the adoption of Attic-Ionic Greek (*koine**), all serve as criteria for establishing a chronology of the inscriptions of this period.

After Philip II's victory at Chaeronea (338), Macedonian hegemony was permanently established in northern Greece, first under the Argead, then the Antigonid kings. Thasos, allied to the Macedonians, saw its political and military importance gradually decline. It nevertheless remained a prosperous city, thanks to its wine exports to the Black Sea and the rest of the Greek world. In 197, by defeating King Philip V, the Romans put an end to Macedonian power. In 168, the Senate abolished the Antigonid monarchy. Two decades later, the

Roman province of Macedonia was created, with Thessalonica as its capital. As friends of the Roman People without being formally attached to the province, the Thasians were, in the 2nd century BC, closely linked to the new authorities. Thasian epigraphy of the Hellenistic period is less abundant and less varied than before: lists of magistrates continued to be kept up to date; decrees, mostly of an honorific character, were still inscribed on marble and on bronze; a new category of documents appeared, that of decrees of foreign cities thanking the Thasians for the benefits bestowed on them. The writing, more and more ornate, is again an important criterion of classification.

13 Theogenes, from an idolized athlete to a healing god (c.390–370 BC) ☞ Room 10

A. *Recherches* I, 9

- at Nemea: boxing.
- at Nemea: boxing.
- [at Nemea]: boxing.
- [at Nemea]: boxing.
- [at Nemea]: boxing.

B. *BCH* 64-65 (1940-1941), pp. 163-200, n° 1

Let those who sacrifice to Theogenes [erasure] deposit in this chest, as a preliminary offering, a sum not less than 1 obol. He who does not deposit the preliminary offering as prescribed above shall have remorse on his conscience. Let the money collected each year be paid to the treasurer of the sacred funds. He shall retain it until the total reaches 1,000 drachmas. When the aforesaid sum has been reached, let the Council and the People deliberate to determine for what offering or construction it will be spent in honour of Theogenes [erasure].

The boxer Theogenes lived in the 5th century BC (c.500–430?). In the eyes of his fellow citizens, he was probably the greatest Thasian in history. The man is difficult to get a sense of, because the documents that tell us about him date from after his own time and they must be treated with caution. The oldest is this catalogue of victories (A), inscribed on a monument in the agora and reduced to a few fragments. Another copy, intact, was discovered in Delphi. It allows for the reconstruction of the parts missing here and shows a layout

Thasos: ten centuries inscribed in marble

in three or four columns: we know that the athlete won two crowns at Olympia, three at Delphi, ten at the Isthmus of Corinth, nine at Nemea, one at Argos – which turned him into a living legend. The inscription of the catalogue is dated to *c.*390–370: it is one of the last Thasian examples of the *stoichedon* style, in which the letters are aligned in vertical lines. At the beginning of the 4th century BC, when concord was restored between citizens, the Thasians chose to reunify around the memory of Theogenes. They went as far as to transform the athlete into a god, alleging he was a son of Heracles,

and to establish a cult in his honour. The fragments of the catalogue were unearthed near a circular altar (★) probably dedicated to Theogenes, who was credited with healing virtues. Near the altar a marble chest was also discovered, on which is inscribed the regulation **B**, prescribing the tariff that had to be paid for sacrificing to the god. In content, the regulation can be traced back to the 4th century BC, but the writing dates from the 1st century AD. This is an example of re-inscribing, which proves that Theogenes' worship remained alive until the imperial era (**28**).

14 Decree in honour of the *Agathoi* (mid 4th century BC)
BCH 131 (2007), pp. 309-381 (*CITh* III, 5), ll. 1-34

[Under the archon* So-and-so. On the subject about which] the polemarchs* [and the ...? approached] the Council and the People [about?... (gap) ...] the agoranomos* *shall not neglect anything [of ...?], the day when (the* Agathoi*) are carried in procession, before the procession takes place; no one shall in any way show mourning for the* Agathoi *for more than five days; no one shall have the right to celebrate funeral rites; if he does, let him have remorse on his conscience and let the* gynaikonomoi*, *the archons* and the polemarchs* not allow this, but let each of them have the capacity to impose the fines established by the laws; the polemarchs**

and the secretary of the Council shall inscribe their names, with that of their father, on the (list of) Agathoi, and let their fathers and their (male) children be invited, when the city sacrifices to the Agathoi; in the name of each of them (= the dead), the apodektes* shall pay a sum equal to that for the holders of an office; let their fathers and their (male) children be also invited to a seat of honour during the contests; the organizer of the contests shall assign them a place and install a podium for them.

For all those who have left behind children, when these have reached majority, the polemarchs* shall give them: – if they are male, to each one greaves, a cuirass, a dagger, a helmet, a shield, a spear, whose value will not be less than 3 minae, during the festivals of Heracles at the contest, and [they shall be proclaimed, with the name of their father?]; – if they are girls, [(the city) shall pay] for their dowry [...] when they are fourteen years old [...] (gap)... If before] reaching the age of [eighteen?] years, [any of the sons?] of any of the men who died [at war?] present themselves before the Council and the People as being deprived of the means of subsistence, and ask for a subsistence allowance, and (once) the archons* and the apologoi*, after taking the oath, have verified that those who have presented themselves (before the Council and the People) are indeed deprived of the means of subsistence, let the prytaneis* receive them and introduce them (into the Assembly), putting to the vote (a proposal according to which) no more than 4 obols will be attributed to each. Let the expense be paid by the apodektes*. (...)

This stele, partially reconstructed from three fragments, stood before the *prytaneion** (★). Dated by its writing and language to the middle of the 4th century BC, it carries a decree of the Assembly, which illustrates the functioning of political and military institutions in the Classical era. The Thasians were then at war and had suffered casualties – presumably on the mainland, perhaps near the place known as Krenides (360–356), the site of the future Philippi (**16**). The decree, proposed by the polemarchs* (equivalent to the Athenian *strategoi*), designates the citizens killed in combat with the term *Agathoi* ('Brave'). It organizes a public funeral in their honour and, in the future, an annual heroic sacrifice. The city also takes care of the war orphans: at the age of majority, the boys are to receive a full set of armour at the festival of Heracles (**11**), while the girls will get a dowry. For destitute orphans, the city even sets up a provision to pay them a daily subsistence allowance. These exceptional measures have known parallels only in Athens and Rhodes. They show that every citizen was also a soldier and had the duty to defend his city in the event of danger. They reveal the intensity of Thasian patriotism and a real sense of solidarity among the citizens.

15 A troupe of young Thasians in garrison (mid 4th century BC)
SEG XXXII, 847

A. *Aetes: radiant, pretty, delightful, full of charm*
B. *Herophon: golden!*
C. *Myiskos (?) and Myiskos, who love the merry bunch.*
D. *My very own Myiskos, delightful!*
E. *Myiskos, the silver Thasian!*

Before becoming members of the civic community, young Thasians – or at least some of them – had actively to prepare for their rôle as citizen-soldier. We do not know the palaestra or gymnasium where they were trained, but we have epigraphic evidence of their presence in the countryside. At the southern extremity of the island, an ancient

tower has been discovered, which may have belonged to a defensive network. Next to it is a cove, where texts are inscribed on the rock face in large letters of the 4th century. They celebrate dozens of individuals for their beauty, in a firework display of qualifiers, half-erotic, half mocking, into which the voices and laughter of a merry troop of comrades erupted. These young men were perhaps performing a military service comparable to the Athenian *ephebeia*, which kept them away from their usual habitat.

16 A tower in the military harbour (*c.*340 BC)
CITh III, 99

> *Herakleodoros son of Aristonikos, Olynthian,*
> *our* proxenos*, *(consecrated) this tower, this exedra* and*
> *this portrait to all the gods, (taking the cost) from the money*
> *he had deposited with Archedemos son of Histiaios.*

Thasos: ten centuries inscribed in marble

During the reign of Philip II (360–336), Macedonian expansion profoundly disrupted northern Greece. After seizing Amphipolis in 357, then the Thasian peraia* (where he founded Philippi in 356), the king besieged Olynthus in Chalkidike. The episode is well known, thanks to the *Olynthiacs* of Demosthenes: after three years of resistance, in 348, the Olynthians capitulated, the city was razed, and the inhabitants dispersed. Herakleodoros was a notable of this city and he had received from the Thasians the title of *proxenos**: his mission was to come to the aid, if needed, of any Thasian staying at Olynthus. In 348, his situation underwent a reversal: he had to leave his homeland and came to Thasos to bring his fortune to safety. A few years later, he offered some of this money to the Thasians to strengthen their defensive system against Philip II. His donation helped finance the construction of a tower protecting the military harbour (★). Inscribed in large and beautiful letters, on a curved block of the tower, the dedication makes clear

that Herakleodoros also erected an exedra* (**22**) and a sculpted portrait – presumably his own. The inscription preserved the memory of a dramatic event, which contemporaries immediately identified without any need to name it: the destruction of Olynthus. It offers an interesting and early example of an individual acting as a benefactor of a city – which in this case was not his own.

17 The cult of Philip Saviour (c.338–336 BC)
BCH 139-140 (2015-2016), pp. 118-123

Of King Phili[p]
Saviour

This modest block belongs to an altar, as indicated by the genitive case (**12**). The owner of the altar is not a traditional god of the Thasian pantheon, but a 'King Philip', described as 'Saviour'. The style of the letters certainly belongs to the second half of the 4th century BC: the king in question can thus only be Philip II of Macedonia. Long-standing allies of Athens, victims of the conquests of Philip on the mainland (**14**) and hostile to his policy of expansion in northern Greece (**16**), the Thasians finally rallied to the king of Macedonia after the battle of Chaeronea (338). Demosthenes alludes to this event in the speech *On the Crown* and points at a certain Aristoleos as the local leader of the pro-Macedonians. This man also appears in the same period in the List of *theoroi**, with his father's name: 'Aristoleos son of Melissos'. The foundation of a royal cult, perhaps still in Philip's lifetime, is an eloquent sign of the political reversal of Thasos in favour of Macedonia, which marks the island's entry into the Hellenistic era.

18 A Thasian victor at Delphi (*c.*340–310 BC)
Revue Archéologique 1948, pp. 705-715 (*SEG* XVIII 359)

Theopompos son of [Melesi]demos,
(having been victorious) at the Pythia *in the contest of the two-horse chariot.*

Praxias son of Praxias, Athenian, made (the statue).

Nothing was more prestigious for a Greek than to win the crown in a panhellenic contest. In the 5th century, the boxer Theogenes, winner at Olympia and Delphi, was the pride of his fellow citizens (**13**). After him, the only Thasian (to our knowledge) who achieved equal success was Theopompos. He was not, strictly speaking, an athlete, but the rich owner of a team of two horses and chariot ('biga'), which he entered into the contest at Delphi, in the third quarter of the 4th century BC. A large base, found in the agora (★), bore his statue. The inscription does not mention the people of Thasos: the monument was therefore, in all likelihood, commissioned by Theopompos himself, concerned about his fame. He obtained for this purpose the

services of a renowned Athenian sculptor, Praxias, who had been settled for some time in Thasos and to whom other Attic-style works found on the island have been attributed – in particular the group of Dionysus accompanied by personified theatrical genres (☞ Room 12).

19 Dedication by a board of *gynaikonomoi** to Aphrodite (1st third of the 3rd century BC) ☞ Room 6
CITh III, 77

> *The* gynaikonomoi* *to Aphrodite:*
> *Kleustratos son of Polykles,*
> *Euxenides son of Diophantos,*
> *Nossikas son of Demoteles.*

Archons* and *theoroi** are not the only magistrates who left an epigraphic trace in the urban landscape (1-4). About thirty bases similar to this one have been discovered on the agora and in its surroundings. The cuttings on the upper surface suggest that they carried marble statuettes. The dedicatory inscriptions show that they were set up by magistrates at the end of their term of office, making an offering to a deity. In this example, which dates from the beginning of the Hellenistic period, three *gynaikonomoi** dedicate an object to Aphrodite – goddess of love but also of harmony between citizens. *Gynaikonomoi** were responsible for controlling luxury of dress and female conduct in public spaces (9 and 14). The office is not attested in all Greek cities. It is characteristic, according to Aristotle, of cities with an aristocratic tendency – among which we must perhaps place Thasos.

20 Epitaph of a slave (1st half of the 3rd century BC?)
L. ROBERT, *Hellenica* VII (1949), pp. 152-153

Manes,
devoted
to his masters,
shepherd.

This modest stele, found at the southern end of the island, at Theologo (★), preserves the memory of a slave. Such 'invisibles' were numerous in any Greek city, but they had neither legal status nor strong family ties nor resources, so they are generally absent from inscriptions. Thasos certainly had a large servile population, consisting of domestic servants as well as agricultural and mining workers. Manes (no patronymic) kept a flock of sheep or goats. It was not his wife or any of his

children, if he had any, who made the pious gesture of offering him an epitaph, but his masters, presumably Thasian citizens, in recognition of services rendered. To judge by his name, Manes was not Greek. He had come from Anatolia along the routes of the slave trade – perhaps from Phrygia, a country of shepherds. Deprived as he was of any education, he would probably have been unable to read his own epitaph.

21 The Milesians honour five Thasian judges (middle of the 2nd century BC)
CITh III, 118 + 119

(Decree) of the Milesians.

It was resolved by the people; the prytaneis* *and the officials elected to take charge of defence proposed: since the Thasians, who are relatives and friends of our city and who are well disposed* *towards our people, sent good men as judges: [So-and-so son of So-and-so, So-and-so] son of Theophiliskos, Ep[i… son of So-and-so, etc.]*

(lacuna of many lines)

[…, So-and-so son of …]eides and [So-and-so son of So-and-so for having …] the lawsuits; and also to crown the [secretary despatched with them, Timoklei?]des son of Satyros with a crown of leaves for carrying out the mission which fell on him honourably and devotedly, [with all possible?] care. Let whoever is responsible for organizing the contest take care of the […] that will be proclaimed (?) […]

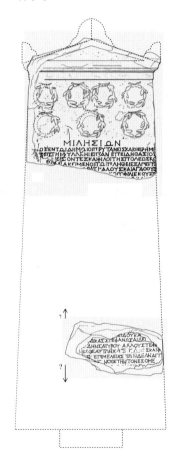

Between Athens and Macedonia (4th-2nd centuries BC)

Commerce, a taste for knowledge or diplomatic relations drove some Thasians to travel and reside abroad. Conversely, and for the same reasons, foreigners frequented the port and the city of Thasos. The inscriptions reveal that the Thasians had a certain international reputation for justice, since they repeatedly provided their services to cities whose courts were blocked or ineffective. Missions of 'foreign judges' illustrate the intensity of exchange that characterizes the Hellenistic period. Some ten cities, mostly in Asia Minor, appealed to Thasos for help in the second and first centuries BC. They granted honours to the judges once their task was accomplished. This fragmentary stele, retrieved from the port, must originally have come from the agora (★). It carries a decree from Miletus ('kin' of Thasos through their common Ionian origin) in honour of the Thasian people, five judges and a secretary – each receiving a crown. The style of inscription points to a date of *c*.160–150 BC. The connection between the upper and the lower fragment is based on the script and on a number of material indications.

22 Dionysodoros, a *nouveau riche* from the Hellenistic period (*c*.130 BC)
CITh III, 108 I

[… ambassadors sent (…)?] to Lucius Aurelius, proconsul of the Romans, (and that), when they came to us (= the Rhodians), they explained to us that Dionysodoros son of Pempides, who is your fellow citizen but who also obtained proxeny* in our city, concerned himself about their safety and their audience with the proconsul and that, likewise, he took care of their return to Amphipolis, and that, in general, on all occasions when they needed him, he showed the most ardent solicitude. Since, therefore, he behaved with dedication to those who were sent by the People, we wish to testify to you also of the excellence of this man and we have appended below the copy of the decree by which the people granted the proxeny*, so that the proxeny granted by the People be also [preserved?] in your public archives.

To the south-west of the agora (★), five exedrae* stand in a row, on which were placed bronze portraits (16). In front of two of them, stelae were placed, bearing decrees of Rhodes, Samothrace, Assos in the Troad and Lampsacus in the Hellespont, in honour of Dionysodoros and Hestiaios of Thasos. These two brothers may have been shipowners with commercial interests in all four corners of the Aegean. The present letter, addressed by the Rhodians to the Thasians around 130 BC, praises Dionysodoros. Thanks to his ships and contacts, he had been of great help to Rhodian ambassadors travelling to Thessalonica to meet the Roman governor of the province of Macedonia. Having thus accumulated honours, which testified to the extent of their international relations, the two brothers had them inscribed for all to see. They present a good example of the important notables who, through their fortune and ostentatious behaviour, came to dominate civic life in the Hellenistic period. As on the two stelae exhibited in the museum (☞ Room 8), the letters are mannered and adorned with serifs (*apices*): a typical feature of Greek inscriptions from the 2nd century BC onward.

In the orbit of Rome
(1st century BC–4th century AD)

In the 80s BC, Thasos was caught up in the turmoil of the Mithridatic wars. Loyal to the Roman side, Thasos resisted with difficulty the siege by the Pontic armies, allied with the Thracian tribes from the mainland. The Roman general Sulla rewarded the Thasians' loyalty by confirming the freedom and autonomy of the city, and by encouraging the consolidation of its territorial hold on the continent, with the support of the governors of Macedonia. The city was less successful during the time of the Roman civil wars (48–31 BC): it served in particular as a rear base for the Republican forces of Brutus and Cassius, at the time of the battle of Philippi (42 BC). After the battle, Marc Antony, during a brief stay on the island, deprived Thasos of a number of territorial possessions and probably also of its status as a free city.

The disgrace was however short-lived: the privileges were restored by Augustus and confirmed by Claudius. The Julio-Claudian era (27 BC–AD 68) saw the beginning of a lasting peace. The city enjoyed a level of prosperity, thanks to the actions of a distinguished generation of Thasians, who, in the inscriptions, bear the title of *philokaisares kai philopatrides* ('friends of Caesar and friends of the homeland'). The monumental centre was marked by the establishment of the imperial cult in and around the agora, and by a number of repairs to, or constructions of, public and religious buildings at the initiative of the same individuals. At this time also, the first gladiator fights known in the region were held, in connection with the imperial cult.

Subsequent Thasian history is that of a city trying to maintain its privileges in the face of interference from neighbouring communities and from the governors of the new province of Thrace, created in AD 46 under the reign of Claudius. The Antonine period (AD 96–192) saw the extension and the monumentalization of the civic centre, to the south of the agora, but also the transformation of the theatre, now adapted for the organization of animal hunts and gladiator fights. In the 210s, a monumental arch was dedicated to the emperor Caracalla on the main thoroughfare of the city, in the immediate vicinity of the sanctuary of Heracles. Throughout this period, and even in the course of the 3rd century, there is still evidence for the persistence of the old established cults. The city also retained its most characteristic institutions, but became increasingly dependent on a group of influential public figures, upon whom new honorific titles were conferred: dedications, statue bases and funerary inscriptions are full of pompous titles such as 'father of the city' or 'son of the Council'.

Thasos seems to have been affected by extensive destruction in the second half of the 3rd century AD. Although inscribed documents became scarce in the 4th century, the ancient city continued to exist and to honour the rulers of the Constantinian period. The 5th century was marked by the construction of the first Christian basilicas, built largely out of blocks taken from disused public buildings of the ancient city.

23 Thasos under the patronage of a Roman (middle of the 1st century BC)
BCH 118 (1994), p. 118, n° 3 (*SEG* XLIV 706)

> *The people (honoured)*
> *Sextus Pompeius, son of Quintus,*
> *patron by ancestral tradition*
> *of the city.*

From the first half of the 2nd century BC, Rome became the arbiter of the affairs of the Greek world, and posed as a defender of the freedom of its cities. Some, among whose ranks Thasos may have been, benefited from a treaty of alliance with Rome, which put them, in theory at least, on a footing of equality. All, however, remained dependent on the new masters of the East, as is shown by the title of 'patron' granted to important Roman public figures. Sextus Pompeius, patron of the Thasians, was probably the son of Quintus Pompeius, a personal friend of Cicero and cousin of Pompey the Great. We know nothing about

Thasos: ten centuries inscribed in marble

the services he rendered the Thasians, his protégés. It is certain that the base, though discovered in the waters of the harbour, stood originally in the nearby agora. Sextus Pompeius is undoubtedly one of the first Romans whose effigy, in the form of a bronze statue, was dedicated by the Thasian people. The title of patron 'by ancestral tradition' confirms that at least one of his ancestors had previously benefited the city through his support. This could be the Sextus Pompeius who was governor of Macedonia in 119/8 BC and died fighting the Scordisci, barbarians of Celtic origin established in Thrace.

24 The walls, symbol of the autonomy of the city
(beginning of the 1st century AD)
IG XII 8, 391

*Sotas son of Euporos, having exercised the charge
of* apodektes **, ordered repairs
on the tower using
the surplus of the city: 7,000 drachmas.*

At the end of the civil wars, the advent of the Principate* marked, for Thasos as for the whole of the East, the beginning of a long period of peace. The military danger had been pushed back to the margins of the Empire, and was no longer a direct threat to the city. The defensive purpose of the city walls became reduced as a result. In the eyes of the Thasians the maintenance of their walls (**16**) nevertheless represented a mark of prestige and prosperity. They also served – together with the continued use of their ancestral laws – as one of the

In the orbit of Rome (1st century BC–4th century AD)

constituent features of civic identity, emphasizing the city's status as a free and autonomous community within the Roman Empire. At the beginning of the 1st century AD the *apodektes** Sotas was thus able to allocate 7,000 drachmas for the repair of one of the towers of the walled circuit, located on the western edge of the city (★). Another sign of a certain conservatism was that the cost of the works was still counted in drachmas, the accounting unit of the city since the 4th century BC, even though the Roman denarius had established itself, from 40 BC onwards, as the only silver coin in circulation.

25 The priestess Komis and the beginnings of the imperial cult (AD 14–29) ☞ *in situ* (agora)
BCH 130 (2006), pp. 499-513, n° 1 (*SEG* LVI 1020)

The priestess of the divine Iulia Augusta,
Komis, daughter of Stilbon, wife of Hikesios son of Aristokles,
(consecrated this) for her (= Iulia Augusta's) entire house.

The clemency of Augustus with regard to Thasos, after the unfortunate episode of the battle of Philippi, contributed to the early establishment of religious honours for the founder of the Principate* and for the members of his family. His wife Livia, in particular, was worshipped under the name of Iulia Augusta. The inscription postdates the adoption of Livia into the *gens* Iulia in AD 14, but predates her death in AD 29. In Thasos she therefore received divine honours during her lifetime, something that was alien to Roman practice – in Rome Livia was deified only during the reign of Claudius – but common in the East. As the wife of the late Augustus and mother of the new emperor, Tiberius, Livia

Thasos: ten centuries inscribed in marble

was the (female) figurehead of the imperial house (*Domus Augusta*). The priestess Komis belonged to an important local family: Stilbon, her father, had paid for repairs to the sanctuary of Artemis; Hikesios, her husband, was part of the afore-mentioned generation of archons* bearing the title *philokaisar kai philopatris*. The inscription of Komis, engraved on the back wall of the great portico located to the northwest of the agora, stood above an exedra*, the very object that Komis was dedicating (★). This monument probably bore a group of portrait statues of members of Livia's family. The exedra* and the portico courtyard which framed it,

on the edge of the street leading from the harbour to the propylaea of the agora, constituted one of the first foci of imperial worship in Thasos.

26 The sarcophagus of Pythion and Epikydilla, archons* and good human beings (1st century AD) ☞ Courtyard of the museum
Revue des études anciennes 61 (1959), pp. 273-299

This is the tomb that Pythion son of Hikesios constructed for himself and his wife Epikydilla daughter of Epikydes. He married her when he was eighteen and she was fifteen; in five decades of common life, they maintained without interruption the noble harmony of their love; they were parents of children who became parents in their turn, twice taking on the archonship for the good of their fellow citizens, good human beings among the living, blessed among the dead. If someone deposits another body here, he will owe the fathercity a fine of 12,000 (staters?).

The beginning of the imperial period saw the multiplication of inscribed sarcophagi, prized by the most eminent families of the city, who discovered, in the setting up of these imposing tombs, an additional means of honouring themselves. Some inscriptions took the form of verse epigrams, as is the case with the sarcophagus of Pythion and his wife Epikydilla, discovered to the west of the ancient city, by the sea (★). In addition to the longevity of their conjugal love, this inscription reveals an institutional peculiarity of the time. Both spouses had been archons*, at least once, perhaps even twice each. The scarcity of candidates capable of assuming the financial burden of the eponymous magistracy had the effect that it became common to take it on twice, contrary to the principle that had prevailed in previous centuries. A number of examples also show that women could take on the archonship, at least in name. The family of the husband, where the names Pythion and Hikesios alternated from father to son, shows a remarkable longevity in Thasian epigraphy, over more than two centuries: one Hikesios son of Pythion was ambassador to the authorities of the province of Macedonia in the 40s BC, while other members of the same lineage appear in colleges of archons* of the 1st and 2nd centuries AD.

Thasos: ten centuries inscribed in marble

27 Conflict of interests on the mainland: a letter from a governor of Thrace to the Thasians (AD 69–79)
Recherches II, 186

L(ucius) Vinuleius Pataecius, procurator of the Emperor Caesar Vespasian Augustus, to the magistrates, the Council and the People of Thasos, greetings. I have done you justice with regard to the colony, and you have received the money due to you. In future, I release you from vehiculatio *expenses, with the exception of those that concern the crossing of your own territory. On the other hand, the decisions taken in the past by the very eminent L(ucius) Antonius could not be called into question. I have given you a soldier; as for the boundary stones, I will place them when I go there, and you will not have to suffer any harm. I have a very strong desire to help everyone [in Thrace?], and you in particular.*

Inscribed on the walls of the building which also bore the List of archons* (**1-2**), this letter from Thrace's governor L. Vinuleius Pataecius, dated to the reign of Vespasian (AD 69–79), evokes a conflict which pitched Thasos against the Roman colony of Philippi, founded after the battle of 42 BC. The subject was the service of the *vehiculatio*, that is to say the transport of the agents of the Roman authorities which the cities had to take care of while they travelled on the main routes of communication that traversed their territory. Taking advantage of an old border dispute, which had already required the intervention of the Roman authorities, the colony had improperly made the Thasians pay the transport costs on a road that must be identified with the via *Egnatia*: by way of Macedonia and Thrace, it linked Italy to Asia Minor. This crucial document reveals the continued existence, under the Roman Empire, of a Thasian peraia* whose boundaries are poorly known, but which bordered on the territory of Philippi and was crossed by the via *Egnatia*. It also shows that a free city could assert its rights before the provincial governor and win the case against a Roman colony in a neighbouring province.

28 Dedication of a soldier to Theagenes (1st half of the 2nd century AD)
BCH 91 (1967), p. 579, n° 26

> *C(aius) Fabricius Iustus*
> *dedicated to the ancestral*
> *god Theagenes*
> *the ex-voto promised by his*
> *father P(ublius) Fabricius*
> *Iustus, while on campaign,*
> *as a token of gratitude.*

Thasos: ten centuries inscribed in marble

This small marble stele, elegantly inscribed, can be dated to the first half of the 2nd century AD. It bears witness to the favour which the cult of Theogenes (**13**), now honoured under the name of Theagenes, continued to enjoy. The epithet 'ancestral' emphasises the Thasian character of the god, perhaps because the ex-voto was promised by a soldier while on campaign far from the city, before being consecrated by his son. For this soldier, the hope of seeing his homeland again was uncertain, and the temptation to put his fate in the hands of the healer athlete was thus all the more important. The author of the dedication, P. Fabricius Iustus, and his son, C. Fabricius Iustus, were Roman citizens with Latin names: to establish their origins we should probably look towards Philippi, where the gentilicium *Fabricius* is attested much earlier, even before the creation of the colony. Whether the *Fabricii* had moved to Thasos or not, the dedication illustrates the fame of the god Theagenes among Roman citizens imbued with Greek culture.

29 An altar for Hadrian (AD 129–137) ☞ Room 8
IG XII *Suppl.* 440

> *To the emperor*
> *Caesar*
> *Hadrian Augustus,*
> *Olympian,*
> *saviour and founder,*
> *and to Sabina*
> *Augusta,*
> *the new Hera.*

Discovered in the area of the odeion (★), in the heart of the extended monumental centre of Roman Thasos, this altar, decorated with a garland motif with rosettes and bucrania, is dedicated to the Emperor Hadrian (AD 117–138) and to his wife Sabina. It is written in formulaic language, very common throughout the

Greek world, where support for the philhellene emperor was considerable. In Thasos itself, two other inscribed altars of the same type have been discovered, as well as an inscribed base and a larger-than-life statue. The epithet '*Olympios*', attached to Hadrian's name since AD 128/9, is characteristic of Zeus, to whom the emperor was assimilated. As a consequence, Sabina was identified with the goddess Hera, wife of Zeus. The qualifiers of 'saviour' (**17**) and 'founder' do not necessarily correspond to a particular benefaction received by the city, even though the reign of Hadrian was favourable to Thasos: during these years, in particular, local coins were struck again after a century and a half

of interruption, bearing the emperor's portrait. The titles on the altar testify more generally to Hadrian's exploits in Greece: he was, notably, the founder of the Panhellenion, a kind of congress of the cities of the Roman East, of which Thasos was a member. On this occasion, the Thasians dedicated a statue of the emperor in the headquarters of the organization, in Athens.

Thasos: ten centuries inscribed in marble

30 A Thasian philosopher honoured by the city
(middle of the 2nd century AD) ☞ Courtyard of the museum
BCH 118 (1994), pp. 408-410, n° 1 (*SEG* XLIV 704)

The fatherland (honoured)
Ktesiphon
son of Nemonios,
philosopher.

The Antonine era was marked in the Roman East by a renewal of philosophy known as the Second Sophistic. Thasos has yielded at least one representative of this new wave: the philosopher Ktesiphon, to whom a bronze statue was dedicated, originally erected on this inscribed base which was found under water in the harbour (compare **21** and **23**). Philosophers and rhetors were public figures at this time, providing education, acting as advisers or spokespersons for their city, even at times participating in the machinery of government, when they were not protected by exemptions. We do not know what kind of thinker Ktesiphon was, for none of his works or speeches has

been preserved, nor do we know whether his popularity went beyond the city's boundaries. At Thasos itself, the social status of his family undoubtedly contributed to his fame: his mother, Komis, had herself been honoured with a statue by the city; his father, Nemonios son of Ktesiphon, had been *theoros** (**4**). It is probable that Ktesiphon himself exercised one or more important magistracies, even if the evidence is lacking. We only have his epitaph, in which his talent as a philosopher, the most noteworthy aspect of his life, is alone remembered.

31 A conspicuous woman: Flavia Vibia Sabina (1st half of the 3rd century AD)

IG XII 8, 389

To good fortune.
The Gerousia (honoured)
Fl(avia) Vibia Sabina,
the honourable
high priestess and, by
ancestral tradition, her incompa-
parable mother,
the only
and the first of
all time to enjoy
honours equal
to those of the members of the Gerousia.

Thasos: ten centuries inscribed in marble

This marble base, originally adjoining the arch dedicated to Caracalla (★), reveals a series of changes in Thasian society in the 3rd century AD. One is the appearance of the Gerousia*: this aristocratic body of elders of the city, composed on the basis of age, but certainly also fortune, had the power to issue its own decrees. They thus decided to erect a statue of Flavia Vibia Sabina, 'mother of the Gerousia': the title is characteristic of the many official distinctions then conferred on public figures, often hereditarily. It was offered in return for the benefactions given by Sabina herself and her family to the Gerousia*. This distinction earned her honours equal to those of the male members of this council. The increased importance of women in society is a further important feature: Sabina is honoured alone, without her husband's name or that of her father being mentioned. Endowed with greater autonomy, women were no longer just praised for their moral qualities, their piety, their virtue, their conjugal love (27), nor for the benefits bestowed on the city by their family, but for their own position: the office of high priestess made them local figures, presiding over the ceremonies of the imperial cult, and probably also the organization of gladiator fights, which fell to the high priests. Sabina has an entirely Latin name. At least one branch of her family was from Philippi, where the *Vibii* belonged to the municipal elite. This inscription reveals a certain permeability between the aristocracies of the two communities.

32 The piety of gladiators: dedication to Nemesis in the theatre (3rd century AD)

☞ Room 12

IG XII 8, 371

> *Euheme-*
> *ros son of Dio-*
> *nysios*
> *to Nemesis,*
> *in accordance with a vow*

Inscribed on a pillar of the theatre's stage building (★), this dedication to the goddess Nemesis, executrix of divine justice, illustrates a cult practice in full development during the imperial period in the world of theatre and entertainment. The inscription is surmounted by a votive relief protruding from a niche carved into the pillar. The surface was deliberately chiselled away: one guesses nevertheless that it represented the goddess standing in front, draped, resting on her right leg, holding the cubit, symbol of measurement, with the left hand. The goddess Nemesis was venerated in particular by the gladiators fighting in the theatre: this was certainly the condition of Euhemeros and the other sponsors of the series of reliefs and dedications to Nemesis that were discovered near the building. From the middle of the 2nd century AD, the theatre had undergone architectural transformations that made it suitable for hosting gladiator fights, as in Philippi and Maroneia. A wealthy Thasian couple had dedicated the construction of a high semicircular marble balustrade, separating the orchestra* from the terraces, to Ares, to all the gods and to the city: the spectators were thus safe from the fury of the men who, at the moment of confrontation, put their fate in the hands of the goddess Nemesis.

33

Statue base for the Tetrarch Constantius II
(AD 324–337) ☞ *in situ* (agora)
Recherches II, 357

> *To good fortune.*
> *Our very great*
> *and very divine master,*
> *the very noble*
> *Caesar Flavius*
> *Valerius*
> *Constantius,*
> *the city of the Thasians (honoured).*

This statue base, broken and then reused together with other bases for emperors in a makeshift wall cutting through the ancient agora, is one of the very few monuments of the 4th century AD discovered on Thasos. Using a very standardised terminology, the inscription honours Constantius II, second son of the Emperor Constantine, who bears the official title of 'Caesar'. In the initial system of the Tetrarchy, founded by Diocletian at the end of the 3rd century

to ensure better control of the empire, two Augusti, sovereigns in title, governed the West and the East respectively, with the help of two Caesares, named to succeed them. Constantius II, elevated to the rank of Caesar in AD 324, retained this title until the death of his father in 337, when he took over the title of Augustus with his brothers. He reigned until his death in 361, first in the East, then over the entire empire. The main significance of the inscription is to show that, in an empire undergoing Christianization, the ancient city of the Thasians remained a living entity, despite a marked decline. Even though it had suffered major destruction, the agora still served as a public space, where it was customary to erect statues of the masters of the empire.

Conclusion

The inscriptions presented in the preceding pages illustrate the diversity and richness of the epigraphic documentation, which makes Thasos, after a century of archaeological exploration, one of the best-known cities of the ancient Greek world. Whole or fragmentary, modest epitaphs or long public regulations, inscriptions give substance to a thousand-year-old story of whose outline the literary sources barely manage to connect the dots. They reveal the everyday structures of communal life – political organization, cultic or economic regulations. They release from anonymity thousands of individuals, with their families, their marriage alliances, their career choices and their strategies of social differentiation.

Many inscriptions were reused or destroyed at the end of Antiquity. Others, still buried under the modern city, will probably never be unearthed. But even if it were ever fully reassembled, this exceptional collection would still give only a biased and partial view of Thasian society: by nature, honorific decrees, statue bases, dedications or lists of magistrates put to the foreground the members of the upper echelons of society, those who occupied the main civic functions and owned the largest estates. An entire section of the population remains in the shadow: the most humble citizens, slaves, freedmen, workers in the city and especially in the countryside, in the quarries or on the farms. Their aspirations, their way of life, their beliefs and all that constitutes a popular culture are almost completely unknown to us. But other archaeological sources can illuminate the customs of everyday life, and can reveal little known parts of this silent history.

ΧΡΙΣΟ
ΔΑΡΑΣΕ
ΘΡΕΠΠΕΝΙ
ΑΡΝΕ̣ṢΙ

ΕΛΕΜΕΝ
ΤΑΡΧΑ
ΡΑΓΥΑΤΑ
ΝΙ

ΜΑΡΚΙΑ
ΝΟΙΟΥ
ΕΤΟΝ

ΓΑΙΣΗΡΑΚ
ΚΙΔΟΥ ΡΟ
Ο ΥΠΟ
ΦΙΛΝΕΧΑΡ
φ

Ε̣48̣η̣

ΝΓΡΟ

ΦΥΓΙΣΗΝΒΕΤΟ
ΝΤΑΠΑΛΟΣ
ΠΕΠΤΑΘΕΟ
ΛΕΠΟΗΕΙ

ΓΑΣ ΕΥΠΟΡΟΥ ΑΠΟ Δ
Σ ΣΑΣ ΕΠΕΣ ΚΕΥΑΣ ΕΝ
ΟΝ ΠΥΡΓΟΝ ΑΠΟ ΤΟΓ ΟΝ ΤΗ ΗΙ
ΓΕΡΟΝ ΤΟΝ · Ρ̄ π̄

Glossary

agoranomos: magistrate in charge of controlling commercial transactions in the agora and of maintaining order in public spaces.

apodektes: in Thasos, magistrate in charge of the public funds.

apologoi: in Thasos, magistrates (7) in charge of judicial affairs.

archons: in Thasos, magistrates (3) with the highest executive responsibilities, and holding the eponymous title, i.e. giving their name to the year.

epiclesis: qualifier attached to the name of a deity and used in worship. Eg: Heracles *Thasios* ('Thasian').

epistatai: in Thasos, magistrates (4, then 6) in charge of enforcing fines and punishments.

exedra: semi-circular marble bench.

gerousia: a council of Elders, which emerged in most Greek cities during the Roman imperial period.

gynaikonomoi: magistrates (3) in charge of controlling women.

hekte: Thasian monetary unit, used in the 6th and the 5th centuries, worth 1/6th of a stater*.

koine: common form of the Greek language, inspired by the Attic dialect, and widespread in all cities from the beginning of the Hellenistic period onwards.

orchestra: in a theatre, flat surface of beaten earth, located between the rows of seats and the stage building, originally reserved for the movements of the artists.

peraia: coastal zone, controlled, politically and economically, by an insular city.

polemarchs: in Thasos, magistrates (5) in charge of defence.

Principate: political regime founded by Augustus in 27 BC, resting on the personal power of the Princeps; it remained in force in the Roman Empire until AD 280.

proxenos: citizen of a city (A) officially charged by another city (B) to look after the interests of the citizens of city B when they stayed in city A; proxeny is both a function and an honour.

prytaneion: building which contained the civic hearth, where magistrates, distinguished citizens and official guests were entertained.

prytaneis: at Thasos, Miletus, etc., magistrates charged with presiding over the meetings of the Council and the Assembly.

stater: Thasian monetary unit, worth 6 *hektai** in the 6th and the 5th centuries and 4 drachmas from the 4th century onwards.

theoroi: in Thasos, magistrates (3) supervising cults and sanctuaries.

tyrant: an individual exercising sole political power in a city; tyranny is a regime characteristic of the Archaic period.

Further reading

The introduction contains a list of the *corpora* in which the inscriptions of Thasos are published.

M. Austin, *The Hellenistic World from Alexander to the Roman Conquest: A Selection of Ancient Sources in Translation* (2006)².

H. Duchêne, *Fouilles du port I. La stèle du port : recherches sur une nouvelle inscription thasienne*, *ÉtThas* XIV (1992).

J. Fournier, P. Hamon, 'Les orphelins de guerre de Thasos : un nouveau fragment de la Stèle des Braves (*ca* 360-350 av. J.-C.)', *BCH* 131 (2007), pp. 309-381.

J. Fournier, 'Entre Macédoine et Thrace : Thasos à l'époque de l'hégémonie romaine', in: M.-G. Parissaki (ed), *Thrakika Zetemata* 2. *Aspects of the Roman province of Thrace*, *ΜΕΛΕΤΗΜΑΤΑ* 69 (2013), pp. 11-63.

J. Fournier, P. Hamon, M.-G. Parissaki, 'Epigraphic research in Thasos, Aegean Thrace & Samothrace (2005-2015)', *Archaeological Reports* 61 (2014-2015), pp. 75-93.

Y. Garlan, *Vin et amphores de Thasos*, *SitMon* V (1988).

A. J. Graham, 'Thasos: the topography of the ancient city', *ABSA* 95 (2000), pp. 301-327.

Y. Grandjean, Fr. Salviat (dir.), *Guide de Thasos*, *SitMon* III (2000)².

Y. Grandjean, *Le rempart de Thasos*, *ÉtThas* XXII (2011).

P. Hamon, 'Études d'épigraphie thasienne, IV. Les magistrats thasiens du IVᵉ s. av. J.-C. et le royaume de Macédoine', *BCH* 139-140 (2015-2016), pp. 67-125.

J.-Y. Marc, 'Urbanisme et espaces monumentaux à Thasos', *REG* 125 (2012), pp. 3-17.

A. Muller, 'Les minerais, le marbre et le vin. Aux sources de la prospérité thasienne', *REG* 124 (2011), pp. 179-192.

A. Muller, D. Mulliez, *Cent ans de fouilles françaises à Thasos, 1911-2011*, Patrimoine photographique 1 (2012).

R. Osborne, P. J. Rhodes, *Greek Historical Inscriptions, 478-404 BC* (2017).

O. Picard, 'Un siècle de recherches archéologiques à Thasos : l'apport de la monnaie', *CRAI* 2011, pp. 1135-1159.

P. J. Rhodes, R. Osborne, *Greek Historical Inscriptions, 404-323 BC* (2003).

Fr. Salviat, 'Les colonnes initiales du catalogue des théores et les institutions thasiennes archaïques', in: *Thasiaca*, *BCH Suppl.* V (1979), pp. 107-127.

List of illustrations

Unless specified otherwise, all photographs were taken by Ph. Collet (EFA).

Map 1 — Map of the island: sites referred to in the text are indicated by a star (EFA, M. Wurch-Koželj, modifications N. Trippé).

Map 2 — The plain of Thasos and the site of the ancient city, including the find-spots of the inscriptions (EFA, J.-S. Gros ; modifications N. Trippé).

Contents

Printed in November 2019

by n.v. PEETERS S.a.

ISBN : 978-2-86958-443-3

Legal Deposit: 1st quarter 2020

Director : Alexandre Farnoux, then Véronique Chankowski – Publishing manager : Bertrand Grandsagne – Editorial folllow up :
EFA, Pauline Gibert-Massoni – Graphic design, prepress : EFA, Guillaume Fuchs – Translation and editing of texts in english:
Victoria Leitch, Riet van Bremen – Translation and editing of texts in greek: Eleni Dimitrakopoulou